Poetry for Your

Samuel Taylor Coleridge

Edited by James Engell
Illustrated by Harvey Chan

SCHOLASTIC INC.
New York Toronto London Auckland Sydney
Mexico City New Delhi Hong Kong Buenos Aires

To my daughter Marleny
and to my son Alec
". . . all seasons shall be sweet to thee"
—J.E.

To my dear big brother Chan Chi-Shing, who inspired me
with his beautiful drawings thirty-some years ago.
—Harvey Chan

ISBN 0-439-63539-X

12 11 10 9 8 7 6 7 8 9/0

Printed in the U.S.A. 40

First Scholastic printing, March 2004

Portrait of Samuel Taylor Coleridge (unfinished) on page 4 courtesy of the Fogg Art Museum, Harvard University Art Museums, loan from the Washington Allston Trust

Contents

INTRODUCTION

Samuel Taylor Coleridge never liked his own name, Samuel. When he was young his family—including his seven older brothers and an older sister—always called him Sam. Later in life, he signed his work "S.T.C." or "S.T. Coleridge" and friends sometimes called him "Coley." As an adult, he thought the initials made his public name sound more brisk and businesslike. With friends, "Coley" or "Brother Coley" made him feel part of a family, which was very important to him. Learning more about his life will explain why.

Born in Ottery St. Mary, a town in southwest England, on October 21, 1772, Sam was quickly introduced to reading, language, and religion by his father, a minister and head of an excellent school for boys. Many times he would take Sam on his knee and talk to him into the night. It was easy to spoil Sam, who was very bright: he could read whole books of the Bible at age three! Sam loved literature and dreaming, and fed his imagination with stories from the Arabian Nights and other adventures.

The happy family prospered. His older brothers were becoming ministers, teachers, soldiers, and doctors. All of them, except Frank, had already left home. Then—Coleridge later recalled the date was October 4, 1779—he had a fight with Frank, who was two years older. He loved Frank, whom everyone thought dashing and handsome, but during a quarrel over some cheese he tried to stab him with a sharp knife! Upset and ashamed, Sam ran away and spent a stormy night lost near the River Otter. The whole town looked for him. When he was found, his legs were so cold that he couldn't walk at all and had to be carried home. He remembered that night the rest of his life.

Two years later—he recalled the date again as October 4—Sam's father suddenly died, two days after putting Frank on board a ship to be cabin boy. Frank was only 11, but it was not unusual then to go to sea at that age. Frank never returned. In just two days' time, Sam had lost his father and his closest brother. A few months later his mother sent him to a strict boarding school in London. He was nine.

All his life Coleridge felt haunted by that date, October 4. He arranged to have some of his plays, books, and poems, published on that date. He wrote to close friends about it when he was thirty, and was still thinking about it when he was fifty years old! He married his wife Sara Fricker on that day in 1795. He persuaded his friend William Wordsworth to marry on that day in 1802. Coleridge seemed to be trying to cope with sad memories by arranging events that represented happiness or a sense of achievement to take place on that anniversary. But he also published one of his saddest poems, "Dejection," on that date. His feelings were full of conflict.

When Sam was a teenager, his family fell apart. Frank, who had gone off to sea, eventually joined their eldest brother John as a soldier in India, but conditions were harsh. They became separated and both died. Rather suddenly, two other brothers died, too, one the night before his wedding. Three brothers were left, but Sam was not fond of two of them, and they didn't like him, either. Then, Sam's beloved sister died after a long illness. His family was shattered. In ten years he had lost six people who had been very dear to him.

Fortunately, after a few very lonely years, he came to like the school he was attending in London. The work was demanding but he studied hard and was successful. School became a second home and Sam made friends there for life. Going on to Jesus College, Cambridge, he won prizes, including one for a poem written against the slave trade. In one very important scholarship competition, he tied for the prize, but then lost it because the other student was slightly younger.

Sam spent too much money, didn't attend his studies regularly, and fell into debt. He left school, squandered the rest of the money that his brothers had given him, and enlisted in the King's cavalry, which was both funny and sad because he couldn't ride a horse! He was miserable. His brothers helped get him out of the army, and Sam returned to school briefly but never graduated. He began to think about founding an ideal community of brothers who would marry sisters. But this plan didn't work out, so he started to earn his living as a writer. He had already published some poems while he was in college.

He soon wrote and sold a few plays. Major newspapers printed more of his poems and many of his articles on current events. For a few years in his early 30s, Coleridge worked as a diplomat in Malta, an island in the Mediterranean important to Britain. He also founded and published two magazines. Each one contains ideas about religion, government, and education that still interest readers. But one magazine lasted only three months, the other less than a year. Coleridge was always writing and was well known, but he had no regular job.

Throughout his life, Coleridge suffered from stomach pains and rheumatism. He also continued to be very sad about his brother Frank, his father, and the deaths of his brothers and sister. One of his own children died, too. To help him cope with these physical and emotional pains, Coleridge took a drug that was very common then, laudanum. It's a kind of opium. People at that time didn't understand that once anyone took it for a while it was hard to stop craving it. Coleridge took too much, and for most of his life he fought against this addiction. Instead of making him feel good, the drug just made him more unhappy.

Coleridge had married his wife more out of duty than love. A good friend of Coleridge's had married one Fricker sister and Coleridge knew that this friend expected him to marry the other. But he found it hard to be settled with his wife and three children. The marriage lasted less than ten years.

Often seeing himself as an adult orphan, Coleridge sometimes didn't have a home of his own at all, but just lived at inns. Finally, for the last eighteen years of his life, until he died in 1834, he lived in the house of a kind couple near London. Many people visited him to hear his brilliant conversation. His friendships with other writers, especially with Wordsworth, were strong and productive. Wordsworth said Coleridge was the most wonderful man he had ever known. But his friendships, too, were often troubled and full of strain.

Friends worried that he did not live up to his own potential, and so did Coleridge. He compared himself to large, flightless birds, or to birds that fly awkwardly—bustards, ostriches, or dodos. Still, he produced some of the best things ever written about Shakespeare; he composed a fine book on politics, and one on religion, too. He fought against slavery and worked to ban child labor.

Even his harsh critics considered Coleridge a genius, or at least they granted that he was capable of being a genius and an original thinker, a philosopher, psychologist, political theorist, and theologian. His public lectures contain some of the best literary criticism in English, but he gave all his lectures, about 100 of them, to earn money that he badly needed. Ideas, learning, and eloquence seemed to flow from his mouth in a never-ending stream. But he had trouble writing down these thoughts in long, organized forms as completed works.

Coleridge's poetry is full of variety. He writes different types of poems in different styles. Some tell stories about strange or supernatural events, such as "Kubla Khan" or "The Rime of the Ancient Mariner." Other poems are written as if he were speaking to us, remembering his childhood, or observing things in everyday life, but with a very sharp vision, such as the way he describes "silent icicles, quietly shining to the quiet moon." If you imagine this, you can see it in your mind's eye. Some poems relate dark thoughts, even nightmares, and others are short and playful, like riddles or nursery rhymes. Only a few poems treat romantic love. So, why is he called a "romantic poet?"

Coleridge believed that unseen forces and powers create everything we hear and see. He thought that a creative spirit is at work in nature and that all of life, all of the environment, is interconnected. His idea was that our own creativity—our power to produce art, to write poetry and music, to dance, to paint pictures, and to tell stories—is part of that larger creative power that makes the universe. Through our ears and eyes—and through the words and symbols of art—we enter into a kind of conversation with nature. We see and hear it, and then we put down what we've seen and heard in our paintings and stories.

For example, in "Frost at Midnight" (page 12), nature is a kind of visible language, a secret book that needs to be decoded. It's as if mountains, streams, and the wind are the letters, phrases, and sentences of their Creator.

In "This Lime Tree Bower My Prison" (page 14), the speaker imagines his friends gazing upon a landscape as if it were a veil through which they see an "Almighty Spirit." The trees, clouds, and even the water "burn" in the radiant sunlight, but they are not consumed or burnt up. Instead, they are part of one larger whole. The everyday things of life can reveal to us what is most precious, even what is holy. But in order to find these things we need to open up our imaginations, we need to go in quest of them.

This is one reason why Coleridge's poetry—and the poetry of other poets he knew and read, such as Blake, Shelley, Keats, Byron, and Wordsworth—is called "romantic": It is about quests, about adventures, but it is not like the old tales of romance, not like tales of heroes and conquests and rescues. Now the quest is inward. It explores our inner being, the secret places of our thought. It explores how our ideas and emotions mix with each other. It explores the puzzle of our own life. But it also looks into the puzzle of the world around us and its mysteries. Romantic poetry is one way to see how the pieces of the two puzzles fit together—how the puzzle of human life and the puzzle of nature cannot be separated.

Coleridge wrote one of the most puzzling poems in English—or in any language—"Kubla Khan: Or A Vision in a Dream" (page 16). It's hypnotic. President Theodore Roosevelt, when he was lost for days in a South American jungle, recited it over and over from memory in order, he said, to keep him from going mad! Yet exactly what the poem is about isn't clear. In a note to the poem Coleridge says the poem came to him in a dream after he took some medicine, but when he woke up he couldn't remember the whole thing. The poem has a curious subtitle: "A Fragment." If it's a fragment, what would the whole be? If it's a vision, does that mean that the whole poem is a vision—like a trance with a secret message—or does the vision begin with the lines, "A damsel with a dulcimer in a vision once I saw?" There is no definite answer. Great poetry rarely gives definite answers, especially about itself, but it does ask definite, intriguing questions. As with most interesting works of art, there is no one correct way to think about "Kubla Khan." It encourages us to be creative ourselves.

"The Rime of the Ancient Mariner" is the longest finished poem Coleridge wrote. ("Christabel" is longer but unfinished.) It has surprising images everywhere, and many famous lines, such as the ones about the salt sea: "Water, water, every where, nor any drop to drink." The poem tells the story of the mariner's soul. He shoots an innocent bird and for his senseless act he and many others are punished. Only when he learns to regard all creatures with a love that accepts whatever happens and doesn't stop loving can he return to the shore. Near the end he asks a priest to cleanse his soul. But forever he is condemned to wander "like night, from land to land," and to tell his story to people who "cannot choose but hear." Readers sometimes assume that the mariner must be Coleridge himself, but the poem doesn't need to be read that way at all.

The best way to enjoy Coleridge's poetry is to read it out loud. You'll hear a kind of unusual music. The rhythm and the rhymes seem at first to be perfectly regular but they contain small variations. The sentences change, sometimes very long, as in "This Lime-Tree Bower My Prison," sometimes short.

Coleridge uses repetitions of words and phrases, sometimes immediate repetitions, sometimes separated by many lines. He frequently uses internal rhyme, words rhyming in one line, not at the ends of lines, for example: "The ship drove fast, loud roared the blast." He matches sounds at the beginning of some words, too: "Five miles meandering with a mazy motion."

All these varied rhythms and sounds produce a magical "symphony and song" that is enchanting (the old meaning of "enchant" is "to be found in song").

Coleridge's reputation as a poet grew during his lifetime and has remained high. Despite some strongly negative comments, even from his friends, readers recognized in Coleridge's poetry great charm, and excitement. In his poetry ideas blend with music and images—images and sounds can stand for ideas. Reading the poetry starts our own active imaginations working. We listen to nature and see the world around us in a fresh light. We blend and transform the sounds and images of nature with our own ideas, stories, and feelings. We begin to work on the puzzle of nature and the puzzle of our own life.

Answer to a Child's Question

People have always imagined that birds have their own language, but what are they saying? When birds mate in the spring, they call to each other, and the lark has a particularly beautiful song.

Do you ask what the birds say? The sparrow, the dove,
The linnet and thrush say, 'I love and I love!'
In the winter they're silent—the wind is so strong;
What it says, I don't know, but it sings a loud song.
But green leaves, and blossoms, and sunny warm weather,
And singing, and loving—all come back together.
But the lark is so brimful of gladness and love,
The green fields below him, the blue sky above,
That he sings, and he sings; and for ever sings he—
'I love my Love, and my Love loves me!'

linnet—*a small songbird*

FROM "SONGS OF THE PIXIES"

Near Coleridge's boyhood home is a cave that is still called "Pixies' Parlour." English legends tell about small, magical beings—pixies and fairies—who live there. Coleridge wrote this poem for some young ladies who visited the cave with him during school vacation.

I

Whom the untaught Shepherds call
  Pixies in their madrigal,
Fancy's children, here we dwell:
  Welcome, Ladies! to our cell.

Here the wren of softest note
  Builds its nest and warbles well;
Here the blackbird strains his throat;
  Welcome, Ladies! to our cell.

VI

Or through the mystic ringlets of the vale
We flash our faery feet in gamesome prank;
Or, silent-sandal'd,pay our defter court,
Circling the Spirit of the Western Gale,
Where, wearied with his flower-caressing sport,
Supine he slumbers on a violet bank;
Then with quaint music hymn the parting gleam
By lonely Otter's sleep-persuading stream;
Or where his wave with loud unquiet song
Dash'd o'er the rocky channel froths along;
Or where, his silver waters smooth'd to rest,
The tall tree's shadow sleeps upon his breast.

madrigal—*song*

VIII

Welcome, Ladies! to the cell
Where the blameless Pixies dwell:
But thou, sweet Nymph! proclaim'd our Faery Queen,
With what obeisance meet
Thy presence shall we greet?
For lo! attendant on thy steps are seen
Graceful Ease in artless stole,
And white-robed Purity of soul,
With Honour's softer mien;
Mirth of the loosely-flowing hair,
And meek-eyed Pity eloquently fair,
Whose tearful cheeks are lovely to the view,
As snow-drop wet with dew.

cell—*cave*
defter—*more skilled*
supine—*on his back*
breast—*surface*
obeisance meet—*proper obedience*
attendant—*waiting*
stole—*dress*
mien—*appearance*
snow-drop—*a white flower that blooms in early spring*

From "Frost at Midnight"

Late at night, when his family is asleep, Coleridge remembers his boyhood and then imagines how his own child will grow up, not in the city, but taught by nature. The poem becomes a blessing and a prayer.

The frost performs its secret ministry,
Unhelped by any wind. The owlet's cry
Came loud—and hark, again! loud as before.
The inmates of my cottage, all at rest,
Have left me to that solitude, which suits
Abstruser musings: save that at my side
My cradled infant slumbers peacefully.

...already had I dreamt
Of my sweet birth-place, and the old church-tower,
Whose bells, the poor man's only music, rang
From morn to evening, all the hot Fair-day,
So sweetly, that they stirred and haunted me
With a wild pleasure, falling on mine ear
Most like articulate sounds of things to come!
So gazed I, till the soothing things I dreamt
Lulled me to sleep, and sleep prolonged my dreams!
And so I brooded all the following morn,
Awed by the stern preceptor's face, mine eye
Fixed with mock study on my swimming book:
Save if the door half opened, and I snatched
A hasty glance, and still my heart leaped up,
For still I hoped to see the stranger's face,
Townsman, or aunt, or sister more beloved,
My play-mate when we both were clothed alike!

But thou, my babe! shalt wander like a breeze
By lakes and sandy shores, beneath the crags
Of ancient mountain, and beneath the clouds,
Which image in their bulk both lakes and shores
And mountain crags: so shalt thou see and hear
The lovely shapes and sounds intelligible
Of that eternal language, which thy God

Utters, who from eternity doth teach
Himself in all, and all things in himself.
Great universal Teacher! he shall mould
Thy spirit, and by giving make it ask.

Therefore all seasons shall be sweet to thee,
Whether the summer clothe the general earth
With greenness, or the redbreast sit and sing
Betwixt the tufts of snow on the bare branch
Of mossy apple-tree, while the nigh thatch
Smokes in the sun-thaw; whether the eave-drops fall
Heard only in the trances of the blast,
Or if the secret ministry of frost
Shall hang them up in silent icicles,
Quietly shining to the quiet Moon.

ministry—*work*
owlet—*small owl*
abstruser—*more difficult*
articulate—*speaking*
preceptor—*teacher*
swimming—*hard to focus on*
clothed alike—*very young boys and girls both wore the same kind of clothes then*
crags—*steep, rocky parts of a cliff or mountainside*
mould—*shape*
thatch—*small branches used to make a roof*
eave-drops—*water dripping from the roof*
blast—*wind*

From "This Lime-Tree Bower My Prison"

After his friends go for a walk, the poet imagines everything that they are seeing. He must stay at home with a sore foot, but soon realizes that nature is everywhere, that we can be open to love and beauty no matter where we are.

Well, they are gone, and here must I remain,
This lime-tree bower my prison! I have lost
Beauties and feelings, such as would have been
Most sweet to my remembrance even when age
Had dimmed mine eyes to blindness! They,
meanwhile,
Friends, whom I never more may meet again,
On springy heath, along the hill-top edge,
Wander in gladness, and wind down, perchance,
To that still roaring dell, of which I told;
The roaring dell, o'erwooded, narrow, deep,
And only speckled by the mid-day sun;
Where its slim trunk the ash from rock to rock
Flings arching like a bridge;—that branchless ash,
Unsunned and damp, whose few poor yellow leaves
Ne'er tremble in the gale, yet tremble still,
Fanned by the water-fall! and there my friends
Behold the dark green file of long lank weeds,
That all at once (a most fantastic sight!)
Still nod and drip beneath the dripping edge
Of the blue clay-stone.

...Ah ! slowly sink
Behind the western ridge, thou glorious sun!
Shine in the slant beams of the sinking orb,
Ye purple heath-flowers! richlier burn, ye clouds!
Live in the yellow light, ye distant groves!
And kindle, thou blue ocean! So my Friend
Struck with deep joy may stand, as I have stood,
Silent with swimming sense; yea, gazing round
On the wide landscape, gaze till all doth seem
Less gross than bodily; and of such hues
As veil the Almighty Spirit, when yet he makes
Spirits perceive his presence.

A delight
Comes sudden on my heart, and I am glad
As I myself were there!...

...Henceforth I shall know
That Nature ne'er deserts the wise and pure;
No plot so narrow, be but Nature there,
No waste so vacant, but may well employ
Each faculty of sense, and keep the heart
Awake to Love and Beauty!...

bower—*a shaded, naturally enclosed outdoor space*
heath—*large area of wild, open land with few trees*
dell—*small wooded valley*
file—*line*
lank—*straight but flexible, not rigid*
orb—*something round: here, the sun*
richlier—*more intensely, more brightly*
kindle—*burn*
swimming—*dizzy*
less gross than bodily—*not so much like things but like spirits*
hues—*colors*
each faculty of sense—*sight, hearing, smell, taste, and touch*

Kubla Khan: Or, A Vision in a Dream

The poem starts by describing the exotic palace and gardens of an ancient Mongolian emperor who conquered China, but then it seems to become a story about creativity, about a holy power that helps artists paint new pictures and poets tell new stories.

In Xanadu did Kubla Khan
A stately pleasure-dome decree:
Where Alph, the sacred river, ran
Through caverns measureless to man
   Down to a sunless sea.
So twice five miles of fertile ground
With walls and towers were girdled round:
And there were gardens bright with sinuous rills,
Where blossomed many an incense-bearing tree;
And here were forests ancient as the hills,
Enfolding sunny spots of greenery.

Xanadu—*Xamdu, a region in China*
Kubla Khan—*Kublai Khan (1216-1294)*
decree—*declare it should be built*
Alph—*probably the river Alpheus, associated with poetic inspiration*
girdled—*circled around*
sinuous rills—*winding streams*

But oh! that deep romantic chasm which slanted
Down the green hill athwart a cedarn cover!
A savage place! as holy and enchanted
As e'er beneath a waning moon was haunted
By woman wailing for her demon-lover!
And from this chasm, with ceaseless turmoil seething,
As if this earth in fast thick pants were breathing,
A mighty fountain momently was forced:
Amid whose swift half-intermitted burst
Huge fragments vaulted like rebounding hail,
Or chaffy grain beneath the thresher's flail:
And mid these dancing rocks at once and ever
It flung up momently the sacred river.
Five miles meandering with a mazy motion
Through wood and dale the sacred river ran,
Then reached the caverns measureless to man,
And sank in tumult to a lifeless ocean:

chasm—*a narrow valley with steep sides*
athwart a cedarn cover—*across and under some cedar trees*
momently—*quickly, suddenly*
chaffy grain—*chaff is the husk of the grain*
thresher's flail—*tool used to separate grain from the chaff*
ever—*always*
meandering—*moving back and forth*
mazy motion—*a wandering, back-and-forth movement*
dale—*small valley*
tumult—*a long, loud noise*

And mid this tumult Kubla heard from far
Ancestral voices prophesying war!

The shadow of the dome of pleasure
Floated midway on the waves;
Where was heard the mingled measure
From the fountain and the caves.
It was a miracle of rare device,
A sunny pleasure-dome with caves of ice!

A damsel with a dulcimer
In a vision once I saw:
It was an Abyssinian maid,
And on her dulcimer she played,
Singing of Mount Abora.
Could I revive within me
Her symphony and song,
To such a deep delight 'twould win me
That with music loud and long,
I would build that dome in air,
That sunny dome! those caves of ice!
And all who heard should see them there,
And all should cry, Beware! Beware!
His flashing eyes, his floating hair!
Weave a circle round him thrice,
And close your eyes with holy dread,
For he on honey-dew hath fed,
And drunk the milk of Paradise.

prophesying—*predicting*

rare device—*unusual work or design*

dulcimer—*stringed instrument similar to a small harp*

Abyssinian—*Abyssinia, in Africa, was thought to be a mysterious country, possibly the site of the original Paradise or Garden of Eden*

Abora—*possibly Mount Amara, a sacred mountain*

I would build that dome in air—*the boast of Michelangelo when he designed the dome of St. Peter's Basilica in Rome*

From "The Rime of the Ancient Mariner"

This is Coleridge's longest, most popular poem. It includes strange, supernatural events but the story is clear. In a senseless, evil act, the mariner kills an albatross, a bird of good omen. The mariner suffers terribly. He almost dies from thirst and sees many others die, but finally he learns how important it is to love all creatures. As part of his lesson, he must tell his own story over and over again.

ARGUMENT

How a Ship having passed the Line was driven by storms to the cold Country towards the South Pole; and how from thence she made her course to the tropical Latitude of the Great Pacific Ocean; and of the strange things that befell; and in what manner the Ancyent Marinere came back to his own Country.

PART I

An ancient Mariner meeteth three gallants bidden to a wedding-feast, and detaineth one.

It is an ancient Mariner,
And he stoppeth one of three.
'By thy long grey beard and glittering eye,
Now wherefore stopp'st thou me?

'The Bridegroom's doors are opened wide,
And I am next of kin;
The guests are met, the feast is set:
May'st hear the merry din.'

He holds him with his skinny hand,
'There was a ship,' quoth he.
'Hold off! unhand me, grey-beard loon!'
Eftsoons his hand dropt he.

The wedding-guest is spell-bound by the eye of the old sea-faring man, and constrained to hear his tale.

He holds him with his glittering eye—
The Wedding-Guest stood still,
And listens like a three years' child:
The Mariner hath his will.

next of kin—nearest relative
din—sounds from a large party
loon—a crazed or simple-minded person
Eftsoons—at once, right away

The Wedding-Guest sat on a stone:
He cannot choose but hear;
And thus spake on that ancient man,
The bright-eyed Mariner.

The ship was cheered, the harbour cleared,
Merrily did we drop
Below the kirk, below the hill,
Below the lighthouse top.

The Mariner tells how the ship sailed southward with a good wind and fair weather, till it reached the line.

The Sun came up upon the left,
Out of the sea came he!
And he shone bright, and on the right
Went down into the sea.

~ ~ ~

The ship drawn by a storm toward the south pole.

And now the storm-blast came, and he
Was tyrannous and strong:
He struck with his o'ertaking wings,
And chased us south along.

With sloping masts and dipping prow,
As who pursued with yell and blow
Still treads the shadow of his foe,
And forward bends his head,
The ship drove fast, loud roared the blast,
And southward aye we fled.

drop / Below—*as they sail out to sea, landmarks disappear over the horizon*
kirk—*church*
tyrannous—*overwhelming*
aye—always

And now there came both mist and snow,
And it grew wondrous cold:
And ice, mast-high, came floating by,
As green as emerald.

The land of ice, and of fearful sounds where no living thing was to be seen.

And through the drifts the snowy clifts
Did send a dismal sheen:
Nor shapes of men nor beasts we ken—
The ice was all between.

The ice was here, the ice was there,
The ice was all around:
It cracked and growled, and roared and howled,
Like noises in a swound!

Till a great sea-bird, called the Albatross, came through the snow-fog, and was received with great joy and hospitality.

At length did cross an Albatross,
Thorough the fog it came;
As if it had been a Christian soul,
We hailed it in God's name.

It ate the food it ne'er had eat,
And round and round it flew.
The ice did split with a thunder-fit;
The helmsman steered us through!

And lo! the Albatross proveth a bird of good omen, and followeth the ship as it returned northward through fog and floating ice.

And a good south wind sprung up behind;
The Albatross did follow,
And ever day, for food or play,
Came to the mariner's hollo!

clifts—*cliffs*
sheen—*reflected light*
ken—*knew*
swound—*fainting or choking fit*
hollo!—*cry of greeting*

In mist or cloud, on mast or shroud,
It perched for vespers nine;
Whiles all the night, through fog-smoke white,
Glimmered the white moon-shine.

The ancient Mariner inhospitably killeth the pious bird of good omen.

'God save thee, ancient Mariner!
From the fiends, that plague thee thus!—
Why look'st thou so?'—With my cross-bow
I shot the Albatross.

PART II

The Sun now rose upon the right:
Out of the sea came he,
Still hid in mist, and on the left
Went down into the sea.

And the good south wind still blew behind,
But no sweet bird did follow,
Nor any day for food or play
Came to the mariners' hollo!

His ship-mates cry out against the ancient Mariner, for killing the bird of good luck.

And I had done a hellish thing,
And it would work 'em woe:
For all averred, I had killed the bird
That made the breeze to blow.
Ah wretch! said they, the bird to slay,
That made the breeze to blow!

vespers—*late afternoon or evening prayers*
fiends—*evil spirits*
averred—*declared, affirmed*

Day after day, day after day,
We stuck, nor breath nor motion;
As idle as a painted ship
Upon a painted ocean.

And the Albatross begins to be avenged.

Water, water, every where,
And all the boards did shrink;
Water, water, every where,
Nor any drop to drink.

The very deep did rot: O Christ!
That ever this should be!
Yea, slimy things did crawl with legs
Upon the slimy sea.

~ ~ ~

And every tongue, through utter drought,
Was withered at the root;
We could not speak, no more than if
We had been choked with soot.

The ship-mates, in their sore distress, would fain throw the whole guilt on the ancient Mariner: in sign whereof they hang the dead sea-bird round his neck.

Ah! well a-day! what evil looks
Had I from old and young!
Instead of the cross, the Albatross
About my neck was hung.

PART IV

Alone, alone, all, all alone,
Alone on a wide wide sea!
And never a saint took pity on
My soul in agony.

He despiseth the creatures of the calm.

The many men, so beautiful!
And they all dead did lie:
And a thousand thousand slimy things
Lived on; and so did I.

And envieth that they should live, and so many lie dead.

I looked upon the rotting sea,
And drew my eyes away;
I looked upon the rotting deck,
And there the dead men lay.

I looked to heaven, and tried to pray;
But or ever a prayer had gusht,
A wicked whisper came, and made
My heart as dry as dust.

I closed my lids, and kept them close,
And the balls like pulses beat;
For the sky and the sea, and the sea and the sky
Lay like a load on my weary eye,
And the dead were at my feet.

An orphan's curse would drag to hell
A spirit from on high;
But oh! more horrible than that
Is the curse in a dead man's eye!
Seven days, seven nights, I saw that curse,
And yet I could not die.

In his loneliness and fixedness he yearneth towards the journeying Moon, and the stars that still sojourn, yet still move onward; and every where the blue sky belongs to them, and is their appointed rest, and their native country and their own natural homes, which they enter unannounced, as lords that are certainly expected and yet there is a silent joy at their arrival.

The moving Moon went up the sky,
And no where did abide:
Softly she was going up,
And a star or two beside—

or ever—*before*
balls—*eyeballs*

By the light of the Moon, he beholdeth God's creatures of the great calm.

Beyond the shadow of the ship,
I watched the water-snakes:
They moved in tracks of shining white,
And when they reared, the elfish light
Fell off in hoary flakes.

Within the shadow of the ship
I watched their rich attire:
Blue, glossy green, and velvet black,
They coiled and swam; and every track
Was a flash of golden fire.

Their beauty and their happiness.

O happy living things! no tongue
Their beauty might declare:
A spring of love gushed from my heart,

He blesseth them in his heart.

And I blessed them unaware:
Sure my kind saint took pity on me,
And I blessed them unaware.

The spell begins to break.

The self-same moment I could pray;
And from my neck so free
The Albatross fell off, and sank
Like lead into the sea.

elfish—*strange, magical*
hoary—*white, shining; the ship is in a phosphorescent sea where millions of tiny sea creatures glow like lightning bugs*
attire—*appearance*

PART VI

Swiftly, swiftly flew the ship,
Yet she sailed softly too:
Sweetly, sweetly blew the breeze—
On me alone it blew.

And the ancient Mariner beholdeth his native country.

Oh! dream of joy! is this indeed
The light-house top I see?
Is this the hill? is this the kirk?
Is this mine own countree?

~ ~ ~

The harbour-bay was clear as glass,
So smoothly it was strewn!
And on the bay the moonlight lay,
And the shadow of the moon.

The rock shone bright, the kirk no less,
That stands above the rock:
The moonlight steeped in silentness
The steady weathercock.

~ ~ ~

The Pilot and the Pilot's boy,
I heard them coming fast:
Dear Lord in Heaven! it was a joy
The dead men could not blast.

steeped—*bathed, covered*
weathercock—*weathervane in the shape of a rooster on top of the church*
blast—*prevent*

I saw a third—I heard his voice:
It is the Hermit good!
He singeth loud his godly hymns
That he makes in the wood.
He'll shrieve my soul, he'll wash away
The Albatross's blood.

PART VII

And now, all in my own countree,
I stood on the firm land!
The Hermit stepped forth from the boat,
And scarcely he could stand.

The ancient Mariner earnestly entreateth the Hermit to shrieve him; and the penance of life falls on him.

'O shrieve me, shrieve me, holy man!'
The Hermit crossed his brow.
'Say quick,' quoth he, 'I bid thee say—
What manner of man art thou?'

Forthwith this frame of mine was wrenched
With a woful agony,
Which forced me to begin my tale;
And then it left me free.

And ever and anon throughout his future life an agony constraineth him to travel from land to land.

Since then, at an uncertain hour,
That agony returns:
And till my ghastly tale is told,
This heart within me burns.

shrieve—*cleanse, purify*
manner—*kind*
Forthwith—*at once*
woful—*full of sorrow*

I pass, like night, from land to land;
I have strange power of speech;
That moment that his face I see,
I know the man that must hear me:
To him my tale I teach.

And to teach, by his own example, love and reverence to all things that God made and loveth.

Farewell, farewell! but this I tell
To thee, thou Wedding-Guest!
He prayeth well, who loveth well
Both man and bird and beast.

He prayeth best, who loveth best
All things both great and small;
For the dear God who loveth us,
He made and loveth all.

The Mariner, whose eye is bright,
Whose beard with age is hoar,
Is gone: and now the Wedding-Guest
Turned from the bridegroom's door.

He went like one that hath been stunned,
And is of sense forlorn:
A sadder and a wiser man,
He rose the morrow morn.

anon—*soon*
hoar—*white*
of sense forlorn—*shocked, dazed*

THE KNIGHT'S TOMB

Sir Arthur O'Kellyn is a made-up name. The poem suggests a length of time far longer than anyone's life. Coleridge experiments with different length lines, 5 to 12 syllables, and with different beats in each line—three, four, or five.

Where is the grave of Sir Arthur O'Kellyn?
Where may the grave of that good man be?—
By the side of a spring, on the breast of Helvellyn,
Under the twigs of a young birch tree!
The oak that in summer was sweet to hear,
And rustled its leaves in the fall of the year,
And whistled and roared in the winter alone,
Is gone,—and the birch in its stead is grown.—
The Knight's bones are dust,
And his good sword rust;—
His soul is with the saints, I trust.

breast—*mountainside*

Helvellyn—*a mountain in the Lake District of England*

Song from "Zapolya"

Coleridge wrote this song for a play. It is a kind of word painting in the form of a ballad, a song that usually has stanzas of four lines each that rhyme a-b-a-b. It is hard to tell if the bird is real or is a vision created only by art!

A sunny shaft did I behold,
   From sky to earth it slanted:
And poised therein a bird so bold—
   Sweet bird, thou wert enchanted!

He sank, he rose, he twinkled, he trolled
   Within that shaft of sunny mist;
His eyes of fire, his beak of gold,
   All else of amethyst!

And thus he sang: 'Adieu! adieu!
Love's dreams prove seldom true.
The blossoms they make no delay:
The sparkling dew-drops will not stay.
   Sweet month of May,
      We must away;
         Far, far away!
            To-day! to-day!'

shaft—*shaft of light*
thou wert—*you were*
trolled—*moved slowly*
amethyst—*the violet or purple color of that gemstone*

From "Christabel"

Coleridge wrote a long, unfinished poem about innocence, evil spirits, spells, and lovers. It is hard to say how the poem might have ended. But reading the start of it creates the dark and mysterious atmosphere of a medieval castle.

PART I

'Tis the middle of night by the castle clock,
And the owls have awakened the crowing cock;
Tu—whit!—Tu-whoo!
And hark, again! the crowing cock,
How drowsily it crew.

Sir Leoline, the Baron rich,
Hath a toothless mastiff bitch;
From her kennel beneath the rock
She maketh answer to the clock,
Four for the quarters, and twelve for the hour;
Ever and aye, by shine and shower,
Sixteen short howls, not over loud;
Some say, she sees my lady's shroud.

Is the night chilly and dark?
The night is chilly, but not dark.
The thin gray cloud is spread on high,
It covers but not hides the sky.
The moon is behind, and at the full;
And yet she looks both small and dull.
The night is chill, the cloud is gray:
'Tis a month before the month of May,
And the Spring comes slowly up this way.

crew—*crowed*
mastiff bitch—*large female dog*
maketh answer—*barks or howls back*
aye—*always*
shroud—*burial garment; Sir Leoline's wife has died.*

PHANTOM

What would we look like if the only things that created our appearance were what we did and what we thought, and not the looks of our parents or any physical accidents? Can you imagine the picture of your inmost self?

All look and likeness caught from earth,
All accident of kin and birth,
Had pass'd away. There was no trace
Of aught on that illumined face,
Uprais'd beneath the rifted stone
But of one spirit all her own;—
She, she herself, and only she,
Shone thro' her body visibly.

phantom—*an image that appears only in the mind, a ghost*
kin—*family, relatives*
aught—*anything*
rifted—*split, cracked*
but—*except*

Reason for Love's Blindness

Even though eyes and seeing are so important to love—think of "love at first sight!"—love is called "blind" when it does not see or think about anything except the person it cares about most: so, in a way, love sees with the heart.

I have heard of reasons manifold
  Why Love must needs be blind,
But this the best of all I hold—
  His eyes are in his mind.

What outward form and feature are
  He guesseth but in part;
But that within is good and fair
  He seeth with the heart.

reasons manifold—*many reasons*

FROM "LIMBO"

Some people believe that certain souls cannot get to heaven, even though they may not be to blame. They go instead to Limbo, a place on the border of hell or heaven, and there they stay, as if time had stopped. The old man seems caught in a timeless trance. He is blind, but his whole being can sense light, and the light gives hope.

An old man with a steady look sublime,
That stops his earthly task to watch the skies;
But he is blind—a statue hath such eyes ;—
Yet having moonward turn'd his face by chance,
Gazes the orb with moon-like countenance,
With scant white hairs, with foretop bald and high,
He gazes still,—his eyeless face all eye;—
As 'twere an organ full of silent sight,
His whole face seemeth to rejoice in light!—
Lip touching lip, all moveless, bust and limb—
He seems to gaze at that which seems to gaze on him!

sublime—*awe-inspiring, overwhelming*
hath such eyes—*eyes without pupils, blank eyes*
orb—*the moon*
countenance—*face*

FROM "THE WANDERINGS OF CAIN"

It was common in Coleridge's time for poetry to describe haunting, beautiful scenes in nature. It was also common to write poetry or to paint pictures about orphans or children who were lost. This produced sympathy, a feeling that Coleridge and his friends thought was important to develop. Here, Coleridge combines natural beauty with human sympathy.

Encinctured with a twine of leaves,
That leafy twine his only dress!
A lovely Boy was plucking fruits,
By moonlight, in a wilderness.
The moon was bright, the air was free,
And fruits and flowers together grew
On many a shrub and many a tree:
And all put on a gentle hue,
Hanging in the shadowy air
Like a picture rich and rare.
It was a climate where, they say,
The night is more belov'd than day.
But who that beauteous Boy beguil'd,
That beauteous Boy to linger here?
Alone, by night, a little child,
In place so silent and so wild—
Has he no friend, no loving mother near?

hue—*color*
beguiled—*convinced*
linger—*wait*

Time, Real and Imaginary

AN ALLEGORY

In an allegory, the characters and action stand for something else. Here perhaps the sister represents "real" time, the passing of time we usually experience, while the brother represents time that we imagine—the past or the future.

On the wide level of a mountain's head,
(I knew not where, but 'twas some faery place)
Their pinions, ostrich-like, for sails outspread,
Two lovely children run an endless race,
    A sister and a brother!
    That far outstripp'd the other;
  Yet ever runs she with reverted face,
  And looks and listens for the boy behind:
    For he, alas! is blind!
O'er rough and smooth with even step he passed,
And knows not whether he be first or last.

pinions—*usually wings, but here arms*
That—*the sister*
reverted—*turned back*

FROM "THE NIGHTINGALE"

A CONVERSATION POEM. APRIL, 1798

Because of the beauty of its song, the nightingale has been a subject for poets since poetry began. The bird often represents not only music and love, but a timeless spirit of free invention, even poetry itself.

king-cups—*a yellow flower, a marsh marigold or "cowslip"*

jug jug—*words traditionally used to mimic sounds in the bird's song*

And I know a grove
Of large extent, hard by a castle huge,
Which the great lord inhabits not; and so
This grove is wild with tangling underwood,
And the trim walks are broken up, and grass,
Thin grass and king-cups grow within the paths.
But never elsewhere in one place I knew
So many nightingales; and far and near,
In wood and thicket, over the wide grove,
They answer and provoke each other's song,
With skirmish and capricious passagings,
And murmurs musical and swift jug jug,
And one low piping sound more sweet than all—
Stirring the air with such a harmony,
That should you close your eyes, you might almost
Forget it was not day! On moon-lit bushes,
Whose dewy leaflets are but half disclosed,
You may perchance behold them on the twigs,
Their bright, bright eyes, their eyes both bright and full,
Glistening, while many a glow-worm in the shade
Lights up her love-torch.

Fancy in Nubibus

OR THE POET IN THE CLOUDS

In Shakespeare's play, Hamlet imagines one cloud to look like a camel, then a weasel, and finally a whale! This poem connects that kind of rich imagination to the creative power of one of the first poets, Homer, who was blind but saw whole worlds with his mind's eye.

O! it is pleasant, with a heart at ease,
  Just after sunset, or by moonlight skies,
To make the shifting clouds be what you please,
  Or let the easily persuaded eyes
Own each quaint likeness issuing from the mould
  Of a friend's fancy; or with head bent low
And cheek aslant see rivers flow of gold
  'Twixt crimson banks; and then, a traveller, go
From mount to mount through Cloudland, gorgeous land!
  Or list'ning to the tide, with closed sight,
Be that blind bard, who on the Chian strand
  By those deep sounds possessed with inward light,
Beheld the Iliad and the Odyssee
  Rise to the swelling of the voiceful sea.

in Nubibus—*Latin, in the clouds*
blind bard—*blind poet, Homer*
Chian—*from Chios, an island in the Aegean Sea*
strand—*beach*
the Iliad and the Odyssee—*Homer's two great epic poems*

SOMETHING CHILDISH, BUT VERY NATURAL

WRITTEN IN GERMANY

In 1798-99 Coleridge traveled to Germany with his friend William Wordsworth. He sent these lines to his wife in a letter. Imitating a German song, Coleridge varies the usual ballad stanza of four lines.

If I had but two little wings,
And were a little feathery bird,
To you I'd fly, my dear!
But thoughts like these are idle things,
And I stay here.

But in my sleep to you I fly:
I'm always with you in my sleep!
The world is all one's own.
But then one wakes, and where am I?
All, all alone.

Sleep stays not, though a monarch bids:
So I love to wake ere break of day:
For though my sleep be gone,
Yet while 'tis dark, one shuts one's lids,
And still dreams on.

monarch—*a king or queen*
ere—*before*

Sonnet to the River Otter

Coleridge recalls the river where he had taken many walks as a boy, played with his brother Frank, and visited "Pixies' Parlour" (see page 10). A sonnet is a short poem that usually has fourteen lines.

Dear native brook! wild streamlet of the West!
   How many various-fated years have past,
   What happy and what mournful hours, since last
I skimmed the smooth thin stone along thy breast,
Numbering its light leaps! yet so deep imprest
Sink the sweet scenes of childhood, that mine eyes
   I never shut amid the sunny ray,
But straight with all their tints thy waters rise,
   Thy crossing plank, thy marge with willows grey,
And bedded sand that, veined with various dyes,
Gleamed through thy bright transparence! On my way,
   Visions of childhood! oft have ye beguiled
Lone manhood's cares, yet waking fondest sighs:
   Ah! that once more I were a careless child!

streamlet—*small stream*
breast—*surface*
marge—*bank*
bedded sand—*sand on the river bed*
beguiled—*detained*

Index